Stephen D. Krashen

Fundamentals of Language Education

Library of Congress Cataloging–in–Publication Data

Krashen, Stephen D.
   Fundamentals of Language Education / Stephen D. Krashen
      p.   cm.
   Includes bibliographical references.
   ISBN 1-56492-088-7 : $6.95
   1. Language and languages--Study and teaching. 2. Language
acquisition. 3. Cognition in children. I. Title.
P51. K67 1991   91-44232
401'.93--dc20   CIP

ISBN: 0-658-01223-1

Published by Laredo Publishing,
a division of NTC/Contemporary Publishing Group, Inc.,
4255 West Touhy Avenue,
Lincolnwood (Chicago), Illinois 60712-1975 U.S.A.
©1992 by Stephen D. Krashen

3 4 5 6 7 8 9 0 VLP VLP 0 5 4 3 2

50000002687595

Stephen D. Krashen

Fundamentals of Language Education

Laredo Publishing

a division of NTC/Contemporary Publishing Group
Lincolnwood, IL USA

CONTENTS

INTRODUCTION

This monograph is a brief description of the theories of language acquisition, literacy development, and cognitive development that underlie current approaches to pedagogy for second and foreign language students. The hypotheses presented are research-based, but I will not present full details of the research here. Rather, I will limit the research evidence to occasional representative examples, indicating where more detail can be found. Following the presentation of theory is a brief discussion of application.

1 LANGUAGE ACQUISITION

The following five hypotheses summarize current theory on language acquisition (for additional detail and evidence, see Krashen, 1981, 1982, 1985a, 1991a, in press.)

The Acquisition-Learning Hypothesis

The Acquisition-Learning Hypothesis claims that we have two independent ways of developing language ability.

1. Language <u>acquisition</u> is a subconscious process; while it is happening, we are not aware it is happening. In addition, once we have acquired something, we are not usually aware we possess any new knowledge; the knowledge is subconsciously stored in our brains. The research strongly supports the view that both children and adults can subconsciously acquire languages.

2. Language <u>learning</u> is what we did in school. It is a conscious process; when we are learning, we know we are learning. Also, learned knowledge is represented consciously in the brain. In non technical language, when we talk about "rules" and "grammar," we are usually talking about learning.

Error correction helps learning; when we make a mistake, and someone corrects us, we are supposed to change our conscious version of the rule. If a learner says, "I comes to school every day," and a teacher says, "No, it's 'I come to school'," the learner is supposed to realize that the -s doesn't go on the first person singular. As we shall see, error correction and conscious learning are very limited.

The Natural Order Hypothesis

The Natural Order Hypothesis claims that we acquire the parts of a language in a predictable order. Some grammatical items, for example, tend to come early while others come late. The order of acquisition for first and second languages is similar, but not identical. It has been established, for example, that the -ing marker in English, the progressive, is acquired fairly early in first language acquisition, while the third person singular -s is acquired later. The third person singular might arrive six months to a year after -ing. In adult second language acquisition, the progressive is also acquired early, but the third person -s may never come. It is common to hear people who speak English as a second language very well, and yet have not acquired the third person singular -s.

An amazing finding is that the natural order appears to be immune to deliberate teaching; we cannot change the natural order by explanations, drills and exercises. A teacher can drill the third person singular for weeks, but as the wine commercial says, it will not be acquired until its time has come.

The Monitor Hypothesis

The Monitor Hypothesis attempts to explain how acquisition and learning are used. Language is normally produced using our acquired linguistic competence. Conscious learning has only one function: as a "Monitor" or editor. After we produce some language using the acquired system, we sometimes inspect it and use our learned system to correct errors. This can happen internally before we actually speak or write, or as self-correction after we produce the sentence.

While the Monitor can make a small contribution to accuracy, the research indicates that acquisition makes the major contribution. Thus, acquisition is responsible for both fluency and most of our accuracy.

Some conscious knowledge of language can be helpful; Monitor use has its place. Acquisition does not, typically, provide us with 100% of a language; there is often a small residue of grammar, punctuation, and spelling rules we do not acquire, even after extensive opportunity to do so. In English, these can include the lie/lay distinction, the its/it's distinction, and spelling demons such as "separate," and "commitment" (how many t's?). Since our standard for written language is 100%, these aspects of language need to be learned, but they make up a very small part of our language competence.

We pay a price for the modest amount of accuracy we get from Monitoring. Some research shows that when we focus on form while speaking, we produce less information, and we slow down (Hulstijn and Hulstijn, 1982).

The Input Hypothesis

The Input Hypothesis attempts to answer the most important question in the field of language education: How does language acquisition occur? The evidence strongly supports a simple hypothesis. We acquire language in one way: when we understand messages, or obtain "comprehensible input". We acquire language, in other words, when we understand what we hear or what we read, when we understand the message.

Comprehensible input has been our last resort in language teaching. We have tried everything else - grammar rules, repetition drills, computers, etc. The Input Hypothesis claims, however, that understanding messages is the only way language is acquired. There is no individual variation in the fundamental process of language acquisition. The Input Hypothesis can be restated in terms of the Natural Order hypothesis. Let us assume an oversimplified version of the Natural Order hypothesis, that we acquire the rules of a language in a simple linear order: 1, 2, 3, . . . The question of how we acquire language can be restated as: How do we move from one rule to the next, from rule 3 to rule 4, from rule 458 to rule 459? More generally, if "i" represents the last rule we have acquired, and "i+1" the next rule we are ready to acquire, how do we move from "i" to "i+1"?

The Input Hypothesis claims that we move from "i" to "i+1" by understanding input containing "i+1". We are able to do this with the help of our previously acquired linguistic competence, as well as extra-linguistic knowledge, which includes our knowledge of the world and our knowledge of the situation. In other words, we use context. (As we will see later, extra-linguistic information that we obtain through our first language can help make second language input more comprehensible.).

The evidence for the Input Hypothesis can be briefly summarized as follows:

(A) More comprehensible input results in more language acquisition. Positive correlations have been found, for example, between length of residence in the country where the language is spoken and attainment in second language acquisition.[1]

(B) Teaching methods containing more comprehensible input have been shown to be more effective than "traditional" methods. This has been shown to be true for both beginning and intermediate language teaching. (See "Applications" section for additional discussion.)

(C) The development of second language proficiency can occur without formal instruction and study. There are, for example, documented cases of adult immigrants developing impressive levels of second language competence without instruction. Also, second language teaching methods that rely nearly completely on comprehensible input have produced excellent results. In all cases of acquisition without instruction, comprehensible input was available.

(D) The complexity of language makes it unlikely that much of language is consciously learned. The grammar of all languages is enormously complex. Linguists admit that they have not yet succeeded in describing all the rules of English, probably the most thoroughly described language. If students can develop a conscious mastery of a significant number of these rules, they deserve diplomas in linguistics.

The Affective Filter Hypothesis

The Affective Filter Hypothesis claims that affective variables do not impact language acquisition directly but prevent input from reaching what Chomsky has called the "language acquisition device," the part of the brain responsible for language acquisition. If the acquirer is anxious, has low self-esteem, does not consider himself or herself to be a potential member of the group that speaks the language (see Smith, 1988b for discussion of this last factor), s/he may understand the input, but it will not reach the language acquisition device - a block, the "Affective Filter," will keep it out. The presence of the Affective Filter explains how two students can receive the same (comprehensible) input, yet one makes progress while the other does not. One is "open" to the input while the other is not.

I have hypothesized (Krashen, 1981) that the affective filter increases in strength at around puberty, which helps to explain why younger acquirers typically do better in second language acquisition in the long run.[2]

Talking Is Not Practicing

Note that the theory maintains that speaking does not directly result in language acquisition: talking is not practicing. If you practice your French out loud every morning in front of the mirror, your French will not improve. Rather, the ability to speak is a result of language acquisition, not a cause.

Speaking can help language acquisition indirectly, however. First, it can result in conversation, and conversation is an excellent source of comprehensible input. What counts in conversation, however, is what the other person says to you, not what you say to them.

Speaking can also help by making you feel more like a user of the second language. For many people, speaking lowers the affective filter. (On the other hand, forcing second language students to speak before they are ready, or forcing them to attempt to use grammatical structures they have not yet acquired can raise the affective filter; for evidence, see Loughrin-Sacco, Bommarito, Sweet, and Beck, 1988; Young, 1990).

2 THE DEVELOPMENT OF LITERACY :

THE READING HYPOTHESIS

Current theories of literacy development hypothesize that we develop literacy the same way we acquire language, by means of comprehensible input. Smith (1988a) and Goodman (1982) have presented compelling evidence that we "learn to read by reading," by making sense of what is on the page.

In addition, there is overwhelming evidence showing that free reading is the major source of our competence in many aspects of literacy, including vocabulary, spelling, grammatical competence, and writing style (see e.g. Krashen, 1984, 1985b, 1988, 1989)."

The arguments for the "Reading Hypothesis" parallel the arguments for the Input Hypothesis that were presented earlier.

(A) It has been shown that more reading results in better literacy development. Those who say they read more, and those who live in a more "print-rich" environment perform better on tests of reading comprehension, vocabulary, writing, and grammar. Also, more comprehensible input in the form of listening to stories is associated with better vocabulary development.

(B) Students who participate in in-school free reading programs such as sustained silent reading do at least as well, and usually better than, children in traditional language arts programs on tests of vocabulary and reading comprehension, as long as the programs last for seven months or longer.

(C) The development of literacy can occur without formal instruction and study. Here are some examples:

- There are several documented cases in the research literature of children who have learned to read and write without instruction, before starting school.

- People who have large vocabularies do not claim to have developed them through vocabulary programs. Rather, they typically acknowledge that reading has been helpful.

- Estimates of yearly growth in children's vocabulary, about 3000 words per year for "average" children according to researchers at the University of Illinois, are far larger than the number of words school programs attempt to teach.

- It has been shown that children can spell many words they have not been taught, and that children that read improve in spelling even when they are excused from spelling instruction.

- Research indicates that readers can pick up small but significant amounts of vocabulary and spelling knowledge from only a single exposure to unfamiliar words in texts. This is accomplished without instruction and without deliberately trying to learn the new words. Researchers have estimated that readers have about a five to twenty percent chance of acquiring a word's meaning from a single exposure, and have argued (Nagy, Herman and Anderson, 1985) that this small gain is enough to account for growth in vocabulary in school-age children, as long as enough reading is done.

The hypothesis that spelling comes from reading is confirmed by an experience familiar to all teachers: Our spelling gets worse when we read misspelled words. Recent research, in fact, confirms that "reading student essays may be hazardous to one's spelling accuracy" (Jacoby and Hollingshead, 1990; p.357). In this study, subjects were exposed to frequently misspelled words. Some words were spelled correctly, and others were spelled incorrectly. Even though they read the words only once, when the subjects took a spelling test, they performed significantly worse on the words that they had seen misspelled.

(D) Many aspects of literacy are too complicated to learn. The difficulties of describing the rules of spelling, for example, have been documented repeatedly. Also, estimates of adult vocabulary size, ranging from 16,785 to 156,000 words, show there are too many words to learn one at a time.[3]

As discussed earlier, the theory maintains that talking is not practicing. It also maintains that writing is not practicing. If you write a page a day, your writing style will not improve. Good writing style, according to the research, is a result of reading, not writing. The evidence for this includes studies that show that increasing reading leads to better writing, as well as studies that show that increasing writing does not result in improved writing (Krashen, 1984, 1991a). Studies also show that people simply do not write enough, in school or outside of school, to account for the vast amount of grammar, vocabulary, and elements of style that good writers acquire (research reviewed in Krashen, 1991a).

Writing, however, makes profound contributions to cognitive development, as we shall see later.

3   COGNITIVE DEVELOPMENT

In this section, I briefly discuss how cognitive development takes place, and then discuss how language can stimulate cognitive development—in other words, how reading, writing and discussion can make you smarter.

We will define cognitive development simply as the development of new ideas (what psychologists call "cognitive structures") and the acquisition of new factual knowledge. In cognitive development, these new ideas and facts are deposited in our "long term memories."

How Cognitive Development Occurs

Both laboratory and informal evidence support the view that cognitive development is not a result of deliberately and consciously attempting to absorb new ideas ("study"). Rather, cognitive development occurs incidentally and subconsciously while we are attempting to solve problems of interest to us, while we are engaged in "critical thinking in specific situations" (Smith, 1988b, p. 53). In other words, "knowledge is a by-product of experience" (Smith, 1990, p.12).

Here are some examples of laboratory evidence showing the reality of incidental learning and its superiority over deliberate study when people attempt to solve problems of interest:

Hyde and Jenkins (1969) presented subjects with written words that were flashed for a brief amount of time, not long enough for subjects to examine the words in detail. One group of subjects was asked to estimate the number of letters in the word (the "count" group). A second group was asked to determine if the letter 'e' was in the word ("e-search"). A third group was asked to rate the words as to their "pleasantness." Hyde and Jenkins then surprised their subjects by asking them to recall as many of the words as they could. As one might expect, the "pleasantness" group remembered the most words.

The "pleasantness" group also did just as well as a fourth group that deliberately tried to remember the words. "Incidental" learning was shown to be just as effective as "intentional" learning or "study".

Wilson and Bransford (reported in Bransford, 1979) did a similar study but added another condition, the "desert island" condition: They asked subjects to rate how important the objects denoted by the presented words (nouns) would be on a desert island. The "desert island" subjects remembered the words better than the group that deliberately studied.

These results are very important. They show that incidental learning can be more effective than intentional learning. In other words, Wilson and Bransford's subjects broke the intentional learning barrier.

It is very easy to break the intentional learning barrier. Many things we do in everyday life, many problems we solve, are more interesting than the "desert-island" task.

Perhaps even more impressive than the scientific evidence are informal observations. A good example is the extensive and thorough knowledge many of us have of our local shopping malls. We know where to park, where the stores are, where the telephones and bathrooms are, etc., and none of this information came from study. The manager of the mall does not give shoppers a manual describing the mall, and require them to get 80% or better correct on a test before they are allowed to shop. We get this knowledge by solving problems —by finding the telephone, by looking for a parking place, by shopping.

Similarly, experts, people with encyclopedic knowledge of their fields, rarely "study." They get their knowledge by extensive problem-solving, and they remember things that make a difference, that help them solve problems.4

We turn now to the role of language in stimulating cognitive development. The research strongly suggests that "smart people" are simply those who have learned to use language to help them solve problems.

And in order to do this, they have had to overcome much of what they learned in school.

We will focus here on the role of reading, writing, and discussion.

Reading and Cognitive Development

Good thinkers, however they are defined, read a great deal and have read a great deal. Simonton (1988), for example, concludes that "omnivorous reading in childhood and adolescence correlates positively with ultimate adulthood success" (p. 111). Ravitch and Finn (1987) in their study *What Do Our 17-Year-Olds Know?* found that those 17-year-olds who knew more, read more. Those who lived in a richer print environment did better overall on tests of history and literature (p. 127). Also, there was a clear relationship between the amount of leisure reading they did and their performance on the literature test.

While good thinkers read more, after a certain point, it is not simply the case that the more you read, the smarter you get (see research in Krashen, 1990). Apparently, it is possible to over-read. Wallas (1926) was aware of this, noting that "industrious passive reading" may interfere with incubation of new ideas (p. 48).

What may be crucial is selective reading, reading what you need to read to solve the problem you are working on now. Brazerman (1985) provides support for this idea. Brazerman examined the reading habits of top physicists, and reported that they read a great deal, visiting the library frequently to keep up with current research literature. They distinguished, however, between "core" and "peripheral" reading, only reading carefully what was relevant to their interests at the time.

What may be the case is that reading is useful to problem solving and therefore cognitive development when it is relevant to a problem we are working on, when it helps us get new ideas or confirms our hypotheses. When we read selectively to solve a problem, we remember what we read. When we read material that is irrelevant, we don't remember it.

Writing and Cognitive Development

As noted earlier, according to the Input Hypothesis and Reading Hypothesis, actual writing does not help us develop writing ability; we do not "learn to write by writing." But writing has other virtues. As Smith (1988b) has pointed out, we write for at least two reasons. First, and most obvious, we write to communicate with others. But perhaps more important, we write for ourselves, to clarify and stimulate our thinking. Writing, in other words, doesn't make you a better writer, but it can make you a better thinker.

As Elbow (1973) has noted, it is difficult to hold more than one thought in mind at a time. When we write our ideas down, the vague and abstract become clear and concrete. When thoughts are on paper, we can see the relationships between them, and come up with better thoughts.

Readers who keep a diary or journal know all about this. You have a problem, you write it down, and at least 10% of the problem disappears. Sometimes, the entire problem goes away. Here is an example of this happening, a letter written to Ann Landers in 1976:

Dear Ann:

I'm a 26-year-old woman and feel like a fool asking you this question, but—should I marry the guy or not? Jerry is 30, but sometimes he acts like 14 . . .

Jerry is a salesman and makes good money but has lost his wallet three times since I've known him and I've had to help him meet the payments on his car.

The thing that bothers me most, I think, is that I have the feeling he doesn't trust me. After every date he telephones. He says it's to "say an extra goodnight," but I'm sure he is checking to see if I had a late date with someone else.

One night I was in the shower and didn't hear the phone. He came over and sat on the porch all night. I found him asleep on the swing when I went to get the paper the next morning at 6:30 a.m.. I had a hard time convincing him I had been in the house the whole time.

Now on the plus side: Jerry is very good-looking and appeals to me physically. Well — that does it. I have been sitting here with this pen in my hand for 15 minutes trying to think of something else good to say about him and nothing comes to mind.

Don't bother to answer this. You have helped more than you will ever know.

(signed)—Eyes Opened

(The Miami Herald, July 22, 1978; reprinted in Linderman, 1982)

Writing appears to have its most powerful effect on thinking when problems are difficult. Langer and Applebee (1987) found that " . . . if content is familiar and relationships are well-understood, writing may have no major effect at all" (p. 131), but when the problem is difficult, writing can have a profound impact on understanding and recall. A spectacular example of this is Ganguli (1989), who reported that asking college students to write three minutes per period on important concepts covered in algebra class had a dramatic effect on their final examination performance.

Additional evidence that writing helps thinking comes from studies of scientific and artistic achievement. It is well-established that good thinkers produce a great deal.

Simonton (1988) provides some striking examples:

> "Darwin could claim 119 publications at the close of his career, Einstein 248, and in psychology Galton 227, Binet 277, James 307, Freud 330 and Maslow 165 . . . " (p. 60).

Simonton also reports that correlations between total productivity and measures of impact (citation counts) are substantial, ranging from .47 to .76 (p. 84) and provides additional data showing that quality and quantity of work are related. While there are problems with this hypothesis (discussed in Krashen, 1991), this also is evidence that writing makes you smarter.

An aspect of the "composing process" that appears to be particularly effective for problem-solving and thinking is revision. Sommers (1980) has confirmed that experienced writers understand that their early drafts are tentative, and that as they go from draft to draft they come up with new ideas. Average and remedial writers don't know this. They think that all of their ideas are in their outline or first draft, and regard revision as simply making a neater version of the first draft. They do not know that in writing "meaning is not what you start out with but what you end up with" (Elbow, 1971).

School teaches us the opposite. School teaches us that we write to display what we already know, not to discover new ideas. In-class essays and essay exams that need to be done, start to finish, in one class period, actually penalize students for coming up with new ideas while writing.

Discussion and Cognitive Development

There is good reason to believe that discussion can serve problem-solving very well. Discussion can provide us with new ideas, help us confirm our ideas, and, as Elbow (1973) points out, can help us clarify our thinking, just as writing does:

"If you are stuck writing or trying to figure something out, there is nothing better than finding one person, or more, to talk to. If they don't agree or have trouble understanding, so much the better - so long as their minds are not closed. This explains what happens to me and many others countless times: I write a paper; it's not very good; I discuss it with someone: after fifteen minutes of back-and-forth I say something in response to a question or argument of his and he says, 'But why didn't you say that? That's good. That's clear.' " (p. 49)

Research is consistent with the prediction that discussion can help cognitive development. Similar to the results on writing research, if a problem is easy, discussion doesn't help; four people working alone come up with more ideas than four people working in a group (see e.g. Taylor, Berry and Block, 1958; Dunnette, Campbell and Jaastad, 1963). But if a problem is difficult, the group may discover a solution that the individual may not find (e.g. Shaw, 1932).

Reports of the success of cooperative learning (Slavin, 1989-90) also suggest that discussion helps. According to Slavin (1987), the reasons for the success of cooperative learning include the following:

(A) Students "are often able to translate the teacher's language into 'kid language' for one another. Students who fail to grasp fully a concept the teacher has presented can often profit from discussing the concept with peers who are wrestling with the same questions" (p. 9). In other words, peer input can sometimes be more comprehensible.

(B) " . . . students who explain to one another learn by doing . . . when students have to organize their thoughts to explain ideas to teammates, they must engage in cognitive elaborations that greatly enhance their own understanding. . . " (p.9). This is similar to Elbow's explanation of how discussion can help clarify our thinking.

Summary

Figure One attempts to summarize what has been said here:

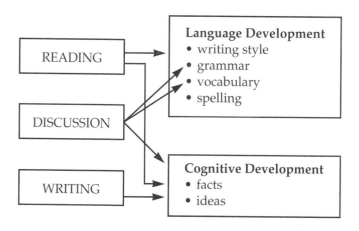

Figure 1

According to the Input Hypothesis, both reading and the aural input from discussion will stimulate language development. Reading, it is hypothesized, will make a heavier contribution to literacy - related aspects of language development. Reading, writing, and discussion will all contribute to cognitive development.

We turn now to the question of what would go to the left of Reading, Discussion and Writing in Figure One. What activities promote reading, discussion, and writing, thereby causing language acquisition and cognitive development?

Free Voluntary Reading

An obvious implication is that any program designed to stimulate both language and cognitive development needs to include a great deal of reading, especially free voluntary reading.

The first step in encouraging free reading is simply to make sure books are available. While it is true that "you can lead a horse to water, but you cannot make him drink," we first must make sure the water is there. Research firmly supports the common-sense view that children read more when there are more books available to them (research reviewed in Krashen, 1987). Moreover, it is highly probable that many children have access to few books outside of school. The first priority must be the development of excellent school library collections, classroom library collections, and the provision of time to browse and read. According to Figure Two (page 25), if all we do is encourage free reading, we will be making a profound contribution to both linguistic and cognitive development.

Enterprises

Besides free voluntary reading, what do we read about in school? What do we write about? What do we discuss? Smith (1988b) suggests that the answer to these questions is "enterprises." Enterprises are problems that students genuinely want to solve, problems that naturally entail reading, writing and discussion.

Finding the right enterprises is, in my view, a major goal of the teaching profession. Some ideas for enterprises in subject-matter classes may include: a chemistry class project in which students analyze the water in the community and publish the results in the local newspaper, writing a history of the community that will become the official history and be on public record, running a small business and keeping the profits, and writing book reviews that remain in the school library permanently for student use, rather than writing book reports.

Certain kinds of games may also qualify, as we will see later.

Good literature teaching combines enterprises with reading, and should thus be extremely effective. Ideally, literature teaching deals with fundamental philosophical problems. It is "applied ethics," dealing with the question of how we should behave. It is "applied metaphysics," dealing with the question of what life is about. Good literature helps us deal with these issues in our own lives.

In a good literature program, students will be reading about these problems in selected works of fiction, they will be writing about them, and they will be discussing them. Also, there is good evidence showing that literature activities, such as discussing stories, can lead to more free voluntary reading (research reviewed in Krashen, 1987).

Note that I am not recommending that all reading in school should be student-selected. In subject matter teaching, many books will be assigned and recommended by teachers. Free reading and assigned reading can help each other, however. In a literature class, for example, the more free reading students have done, the more they will appreciate good literature. On the other hand, a successful literature class will result in more free reading.

Figure Two expands Figure One, adding enterprises and free reading. An important characteristic of Figure Two is that the arrows go from left to right, not from right to left. As Smith (1988b) has pointed out, we have confused cause and effect in education. We do not learn parts of language and "facts" so that we can eventually read and work on problems. We read for interest and pleasure and engage in problem-solving, and language acquisition and intellectual development occur as a result.

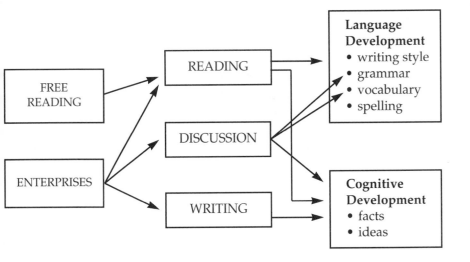

Figure 2

4   APPLICATIONS

Beginning Language Teaching

Methods such as Asher's Total Physical Response Method (Asher, 1988) and Terrell's Natural Approach (Krashen and Terrell, 1983) provide students with aural comprehensible input and are an ideal start in language acquisition. I focus here on Natural Approach.

Natural Approach classes are organized thematically, around topics and activities that students in a particular class will find interesting and comprehensible. Thus, a Natural Approach activity that might work for a university-level French course may not work in a third-grade ESL class, and vice-versa.

Natural Approach does not use a grammatical syllabus, not even one based on the "natural order." It has been argued (Krashen, 1982) that comprehensible input, if there is enough of it, automatically contains the grammar that students are ready to acquire. In other words, "i+l" (see earlier discussion of the Input hypothesis) is present in comprehensible input. This, of course, makes it easier to make activities interesting. (It is very hard to say things that are interesting and comprehensible, when the "hidden agenda" of an activity is a particular rule of grammar, such as the relative clause.) Using a thematic approach also helps teachers handle, within reason, individual variation, the fact that in the same class there may be different students may be ready to understand different rules. Given enough comprehensible input, everyone will get "i+l", even though "i+l" could be different for each person in the class.

Natural Approach teachers help make input comprehensible by providing extra-linguistic knowledge in the form of pictures and realia, and by modifying their speech. The adjustments they make, however, are not rigidly imposed. Rather, teachers naturally tend to talk a little slower and use somewhat less complex language as they try to make themselves understood.

Natural Approach activities attempt to be of genuine interest to the students. They include discussions of topics of interest, games, and problem-solving activities. Brown and Palmer (1988) suggest some very interesting activities for beginning language classes: Magic tricks, simple scientific experiments, playing darts, playing card games, learning to do a headstand, etc. Their suggestions illustrate the freedom Natural Approach teachers have. All that is required is that the activity be interesting and comprehensible. There is no requirement that the activity provide practice with a particular grammatical structure, since, given enough comprehensible input, "i+l" is automatically included.

In Natural Approach, there is, at first, little demand for student output. Beginning students are able to fully participate in activities while saying nothing, or by saying very little. When they speak, complete sentences are not required, and errors are not corrected (for a review of the research showing the futility of error correction, see Krashen, 1991a, in press).

Grammar is included in Natural Approach, only for older students (high school and older), and only as a supplementary activity. Grammar is included for two reasons:

(1) to satisfy the curiosity some students have about the structure of language - in other words, as linguistics.

(2) to fill in some of the gaps left by acquisition.

As noted earlier, acquisition will give us nearly all of a language, but not 100%. Unfortunately, writing that is intended to be read by other people must be 100% accurate. Natural Approach provides, therefore, for the conscious learning of rules that many people, despite extensive reading, do not acquire. Such rules should be used when they do not interfere with communication, as in the editing stage of composing. It is <u>not</u> expected that rules "learned" in the grammar activities will be available for spontaneous use in conversation. There is no expectation, in other words, that "learned" grammar rules will become "acquired".

Research on Natural Approach and other beginning comprehensible-input-based methods confirms their effectiveness. Students in these classes typically outperform traditionally taught students on tests involving real communication. On grammar tests, there is usually no difference. In other words, there is nothing lost. (For reviews of this research, see Krashen, 1982, in press.)

Limits of Beginning Methods

As effective as Natural Approach is, it is not enough. Methods such as Natural Approach provide "conversational" language. Second language students need more: they need advanced or "academic" language proficiency (Cummins, 1981). It has been shown that conversational language does not make a large contribution to academic success among language minority students (Cummins, 1981; Saville-Troike, 1984). In fact, language minority students typically acquire conversational language anyway (see e.g. research described in Krashen and Biber, 1988). Methods such as Natural Approach will speed up the process of acquiring conversational language, and are thus of great help, but they are not the solution to the problem.

Conversational language is also not enough to allow the foreign language student to read the classics, engage in the serious study of literature, use the language for international business, or do advanced scholarship.

There are at least two aspects of advanced or academic language:

(1) the code itself, the style associated with education. This means a wide vocabulary, complex grammar, and correct use of the conventions of writing;

(2) the ability to use language to solve problems and stimulate cognitive development.

In the sections that follow, three ways will be presented for attaining competence in academic language:

(1) free reading,
(2) sheltered subject-matter teaching and
(3) the proper use of the student's first language.

Free Reading

As argued earlier, free reading is an extremely powerful way of promoting both language development and cognitive development. Good libraries, good literature programs, and sustained silent reading are all well-established ways of promoting reading. Reading can be integrated into nearly all parts of the curriculum; in social studies classes, for example, students can supplement the regular text by choosing from historical novels, novels dealing with social issues, and biographies, reading experiences that will broaden their knowledge of social studies and that may inspire them to do additional reading of this kind on their own.

When a student is well-read, s/he cannot help but absorb nearly all the conventions of writing that the public is so concerned about. S/he will write well , and write correctly simply because s/he has no choice, because appropriate style and mastery of spelling and mechanics have, to a large extent, been subconsciously acquired.

Sheltered Subject Matter Teaching

Inspired by the success of Canadian immersion programs (see e.g. Lambert and Tucker, 1972), Sheltered Subject Matter Teaching (SSMT) derives from one important concept: subject matter teaching in a second language, when it is comprehensible, is language teaching, because it provides comprehensible input.

Typically in SSMT, only second language acquirers are allowed in the class. When all students are second language acquirers, when all students are in the same linguistic boat, it is easier for the teacher to make the input comprehensible.

A crucial characteristic of SSMT is that both students and teacher are focused on subject matter, not language. This emphasis on meaning, not form, results in more comprehensible input, and thus more language acquisition. Sheltered subject matter classes are thus not "ESL Math" or "ESL History" but are "math" and "history". Research on SSMT has shown that students in these classes acquire considerable amounts of the second language, doing at least as well as students in regular language classes, and also learn impressive amounts of subject matter. Thus, SSMT is very time-efficient; students get both language and subject matter knowledge at the same time. Also, SSMT provides exposure to just the kind of language students will need to survive in the academic mainstream.

New Directions in SSMT

SSMT has been successfully applied to much of the elementary school curriculum (Swain and Lapkin, 1982), and to subject matter at the university level. Sheltered students have learned psychology (Edwards et. al., 1984; Hauptman et. al., 1988), culture and civilization (Sternfeld, 1989; Lafayette and Buscaglia, 1985), economics (Schleppegrell, 1984), social work (Peck, 1987), and applied linguistics (Buch and de Bagheera, 1978; Milk, 1990) in SSMT.

I have discussed some other possibilities for sheltered courses for foreign and second language students elsewhere (Krashen, 1982, 1985a).

Some of the most promising areas for sheltered subject matter teaching that would be usable for all levels are courses in popular literature and the use of games. Popular literature and games promise to provide a wide variety of input, using activities that students find not merely interesting but often compelling.

Popular Literature

Including a sheltered popular literature class may be a good way to combine pleasure reading and sheltered subject matter instruction, two very effective means of moving beyond conversational language.

The goal of a popular literature class is to introduce students to many kinds of popular literature, so that eventually students will read on their own. This includes comic books (for students of all ages; for a review of the research, Krashen, 1989b), magazines (Rucker, 1982), newspapers, and popular novels.

Such a class will also give students a considerable amount of information about the everyday culture of the speakers of the target language, as well as linguistic competence.

A popular literature course can be followed by an individualized reading course. In individualized reading, students are given a chance to read extensively in an area of their own interest. Appleby and Conner (1965) provide an excellent description of an elective individualized reading course for high school students in their first language, and many of their suggestions can easily be used in a sheltered second or foreign language class.

Since free voluntary reading makes such a powerful contribution to language development, it would be helpful if students could take an individualized reading course for credit more than once.

Games

According to the theories of language acquisition and cognitive development presented earlier, several kinds of advanced games should be very effective at the intermediate level, games that require difficult problem-solving, and that involve discussion, and in some cases reading and writing.

Straight forward board games promote interaction, and have the potential of supplying some subject matter knowledge; *Britannia* (Avalon Hill Game Co.), for example, is a challenging game that takes place in Britain in the first century. While playing, participants inevitably learn a great deal of social science and history.

The fullest potential of games is reached in what are termed "role-playing games," extremely complex games which require demanding solitary reading for character creation, and extensive group interaction in playing the actual game. The best known of the role-playing games is Dungeons and Dragons, but many variants exist, including some that set their adventures in actual historical locations, such as the *China* and *Vikings* modules from the GURP (Generic Universal Role Playing) system. Playing these games can result in significant subject-matter learning as well as language acquisition.

While there has been no evaluation of the value of role - playing games in language acquisition, it is a safe bet that they will be effective. Role - playing games provide input through reading, as well as input through interaction, and research suggests that interaction is extremely helpful in making input comprehensible (e.g. Pica, Young, and Doughty, 1987). In addition, Rhoda McGraw and Sian Howells have been offering role-playing games as part of advanced English as a Foreign Language at the Ecole Nationale des Pont et Chassees in Paris, with great apparent success.

Role - playing games meet what Slavin (1987, 1989- 90) considers the essential requirements of cooperative learning: participants are working toward a common goal, and each individual makes a contribution. Since cooperative learning has been shown to be effective in promoting cognitive development (Slavin, 1987, 1989 - 90; see also the section on "Discussion" above), it is a reasonable conclusion that role - playing games will also stimulate cognitive development (see also Bejarano, 1987, for evidence that cooperative learning is beneficial for second language acquisition).

An obvious problem with games, as with all interaction activities, is that students hear primarily the speech of other students, or "inter-language talk" (Krashen, 1981). I have argued that inter-language talk probably does more good than harm, but if students hear only inter-language talk, there is some chance they may acquire the errors they hear, leading to "fossilization" (Krashen, 1985a). The cure for this is to include native speakers in the games. Including native speakers as game participants violates one of the principles of sheltered subject matter teaching, but is consistent with a deeper principle: comprehensible input. When native speakers are in the game, their input can be highly comprehensible; much of what they say will be related to the game. Thus, second language students will have background knowledge to help them understand the native speaker input.

For second language acquisition, finding participants is not a problem, since enthusiastic gamers are present on all school and university campuses. For foreign language situations, native speakers may be harder to find, but when they are available, their task in the classroom will be obvious, simply to participate in the game.

Linguistics

Another area of SSMT that is still unexplored is the use of a sheltered course in linguistics dealing with the structure of the target language, its history and dialects, and the structure of closely related languages.

In addition, if we are interested in students' continuing to improve on their own, we should consider sharing information with them about language acquisition, and the relevance of this information to language pedagogy and their own progress in acquiring a second language. [5]

5   Why Bilingual Education?`

The Use of the Student's First Language

When the first language is used correctly in educational programs, it is of tremendous benefit. It can catalyze and accelerate second language acquisition. When it is used incorrectly, it is harmful. It can slow down second language acquisition.

By one of life's happy coincidences, the right way of using the student's first language is the easy way, and the wrong way is the hard way.

We first need to consider how first language education can help second language development. Common sense seems to tell us the opposite, that the more a student hears a language, the faster s/he will acquire it. It turns out that this is not the case. We will see, in fact, that the principles supporting good bilingual education are the same principles underlying language acquisition and cognitive development presented earlier.

When we give students good instruction through their first language, we give them two things. First, we give them knowledge. This can be subject-matter knowledge, or knowledge of the world in general.

The knowledge that the students get in their first language can make second language input much more comprehensible. A child who is at grade level in math, for example, thanks to quality education in his/her first language, will be able to follow a math class taught in the second language much better than a child who is behind in math. The first child will not only get more math, s/he will make more progress in second language acquisition, because s/he will get more comprehensible input.

Second, quality education in the primary language helps the student develop literacy in the second language. We can distinguish two kinds of literacy:

(A) What we can call "basic" literacy, the ability to read and write. Showing how the first language helps develop basic literacy is a two-step argument:

If, as claimed earlier, we learn to read by reading, it will be much easier to learn to read in a language you know, since the print in that language will be more comprehensible.

Once you can read, you can read. This ability transfers rapidly to other languages you acquire. And, as we have seen, reading is the way we develop other literacy - related aspects of linguistic competence.

The goal is second language literacy. A rapid means of achieving it is building reading ability in the first language.

(B) The second kind of literacy is the kind discussed in chapter 3, the ability to use language, oral and written, to solve problems and make yourself smarter. Clearly, this kind of competence also transfers across languages. If you have learned, for example, to read selectively or have learned that revision helps you discover new ideas in one language, you will be able to read selectively and revise your writing in another language. In other words, once you are educated, you are educated.

If these principles are correct, they suggest that quality programs for second language acquirers will have the following characteristics:

- They will supply comprehensible input in the second language, in the form of good beginning language classes, sheltered subject matter teaching, and a print-rich environment in the second language.

- They will provide quality subject matter teaching in the first language, without translation. This will give the second language acquirer background information that will make second language input more comprehensible.

- They will help the student develop literacy in the first language, through free reading and effective language arts programs, literacy that will transfer to the second language .

Striking evidence showing that these characteristics are correct is the finding that programs for language minority students in the United States that conform to these characteristics teach English and subject matter very well, just as well as, and often better than, all-day English programs. These results have been confirmed often in the professional literature (for reviews, see Cummins, 1981, 1984; Willig, 1985; Krashen and Biber, 1988; for a discussion of some current controversies in the research, see Krashen, 1991b; for some programmatic suggestions, see Krashen, 1985a; Krashen and Biber, 1988).6

It generally takes some time for limited English proficient children to reach grade norms in tests of academic English (usually about five to eight years for children not in bilingual education programs; Cummins, 1981; Collier, 1987). Cummins (1981) explains why: The native English speaking children are not standing still. They are making impressive gains; as we learned earlier, they are acquiring, for example, about 3000 new words each year. Language minority students in well-designed programs reach grade norms at least as quickly as those in non-bilingual programs, and usually do better (e.g. Krashen and Biber, 1988). They are clearly accomplishing a remarkable feat. They are catching up to native speakers, a moving target, and are developing their first language as well.

Doing It Wrong

Not all bilingual programs are effective. One kind that has been shown to be ineffective is "concurrent translation," a method in which the teacher speaks in one language, and then translates what was said into the other language. This method is exhausting in addition to being ineffective (Legarreta, 1979; Wong-Fillmore, 1975). The Input Hypothesis helps explain why it doesn't work; when teachers use concurrent translation, the student doesn't have to listen to the second language, and the teacher doesn't need to attempt to make the second-language input comprehensible.

The generalization is simple: when we use the first language to supply background knowledge and literacy, it helps. When we use it for translation, it doesn't help.

Advanced First Language Development

The arguments presented thus far are for first language development in the earlier years. There are also excellent arguments for advanced first language development. Research suggests that advanced first language development has some cognitive advantages (see e.g. Hakuta, 1986); those who attain advanced levels of proficiency in both languages do somewhat better on tests of cognitive flexibility (divergent thinking) and on certain linguistic tests. Also, there are practical job-related advantages to high levels of bilingualism (Simon, 1980).

Finally, bilingualism helps to promote a healthy sense of biculturalism and avoid the syndrome of "bicultural ambivalence," shame of the first culture and hostility towards the second culture (Cummins, 1981); good bilingual programs can raise the prestige of the first culture, which will raise the child's self-esteem and thereby lower the affective filter, resulting in better adjustment and better second language acquisition.

For these reasons, it appears to be the case that proper bilingual education is a "good deal" for both the individual student as well as the culture s/he is living in.

Notes

1. Living in the country where the language is spoken is of greatest benefit to students who can understand at least some of what they hear and read. Beginners benefit less from living in the country. Language classrooms are of great help to beginners, since classes give them the comprehensible input that the "outside world" gives them only reluctantly. The goal of the class is to bring students to the level where they can understand some of the input they encounter outside of class.

2. But older acquirers are faster in the short run; (see e.g. Krashen, Long and Scarcella, 1979.) The child's superiority in second-language acquisition has, in my opinion, been overrated. Adult second-language acquirers who live in an input-rich second-language environment may not achieve total perfection, but they often do very well in second-language acquisition, acquiring nearly all of a very complex system.

3. 16,785 is the lowest known estimate of adult vocabulary size. To arrive at this figure, researchers had to eliminate hyphenated words (e.g. free-lance), capitalized words, foreign words, words "identified as old use" (e.g. forsooth) letters and names of letters (alpha), abbreviations, slang, and "multi-word entries" (e.g. video cassette) (D'Anna, Zechmeister, and Hall, 1991).

4. It could be argued that experts only become experts because of their academic success, which is assumed to be based on study. Academic success and real - world accomplishment are not directly related, however. Simonton (1984) presents strong empirical evidence supporting the view that some education is useful, but "the development of creative potential may be weakened by excessive formal training...the more impressive intellects simply may not need a doctorate" (p.73). In addition, Bloom (1963) reported that former graduate students at the University of Chicago who went on to successful research careers after the Ph.D. were not necessarily those with better grades, but were those who had a "preoccupation with problems rather than with the subject matter of courses." They were those who completely accepted "the role of research worker and scholar (rather than the role of student) " (pp. 257 -58).

5. B. Elbaum (personal communication) has suggested that the university foreign language requirement simply be passing a sheltered subject-matter course. This is a very sensible idea, in that it will demonstrate that the student can use the second language to learn new information, and will, as Sternfeld (1989) has noted, entail gaining a great deal of cultural knowledge.

6. Note also that children who do well without bilingual education are typically those who are well-educated in their own language. They have had subject- matter teaching and literacy development in their primary language, two of the three characteristics of an effective program.

REFERENCES

Appleby, B. and Conner, J. 1965. " Well, what did you think of it?" *English Journal* 54: 606-612.

Asher, J. 1988. *Learning Another Language through Actions: The Complete Teacher's Guidebook.* Los Gatos, California: Sky Oaks Productions.

Bejarano, Y. 1987. "A cooperative small-group methodology in the language classroom." TESOL *Quarterly* 21: 483-504.

Bransford, J. 1979. *Human Cognition: Learning, Understanding, and Remembering.* Belmon, Ca.: Wadsworth.

Brazerman, C. 1985. "Physicists reading physics: Schema-laden purposes and purpose-laden schema." *Written Communication* 2: 3-43.

Brown, M. and Palmer, A. 1987. *The Listening Approach.* New York: Longman.

Buch, G. and I. de Bagheera. 1978. "An immersion program for the professional improvement of non-native teachers of ESL". In C. Blatchford and J. Schachter (Eds.) *On* TESOL'78. Washington: TESOL, pp. 106-117.

Collier, V. 1987. "Age and rate of acquisition of second language for academic purposes." TESOL *Quarterly* 21: 617-641.

Cummins, J. 1981. "The role of primary language development in promoting success for language minority students." In Office of Bilingual Education, State of California (Eds.) *Schooling and Language Minority Students: A Theoretical Framework.* California State University, Los Angeles: Evaluation, Dissemination and Assessment Center, pp. 3-49.

Cummins, J. 1984. *Bilingualism and Special Education: Issues in Assessment and Pedagogy.* Clevedon, Avon, England: Multilingual Matters.

D'Anna, C., Zechmeister, E., and Hall, J. 1991. "Toward a meaningful definition of vocabulary size." *Journal of Reading Behavior* 23: 109-122.

Dunnette, M., Campbell, J. and Jaastad, K. 1963. "The effect of group participation on brain-storming effectiveness for two industrial samples." *Journal of Applied Psychology* 47: 30-37.

Edwards, H., Wesche, M., Krashen, S., Clement, R., and Kruidenierr, B. 1985. "Second-language acquisition through subject-matter learning: A study of sheltered psychology classes at the University of Ottawa." *The Canadian Modern Language Review* 41: 268-282.

Elbow, P. 1973. *Writing without Teachers.* New York: Oxford University Press.

Elbow, P. 1981. *Writing with Power.* New York: Oxford University Press.

Ganguli, A. 1989. "Integrating writing in developmental mathematics." *College Teaching* 37: 140-142.

Goodman, K. 1982. *Language and Literacy: The Selected Writings of Kenneth S. Goodman.* Ed. F. Gollasch. London: Routledge and Kegan Paul.

Hakuta, K. 1986. *Mirror of Language: The Debate on Bilingualism.* New York: Basic Books.

Hyde, T. and Jenkins, J. 1969. "Differential effects of incidental tasks on the organization of recall of a list of highly associated words." *Journal of Experimental Psychology* 82: 472-81.

Hauptman, P., Wesche, M., and Ready, D. 1988. "Second-language acquisition through subject matter learning: A follow-up study at the University of Ottawa". *Language Learning* 38: 433-471.

Hulstijn, J. and Hulstijn, W. 1984. " Grammatical errors as a function of processing constraints and explicit knowledge." *Language Learning* 34: 23-43.

Jacoby, L. and Hollingshead, A. 1990. "Reading student essays may be hazardous to your spelling: Effects of reading incorrectly and correctly spelled words." *Canadian Journal of Psychology* 44: 345-358.

Krashen, S. 1981. *Second Language Acquisition and Second Language Learning.* New York: Prentice Hall.

Krashen, S. 1982. *Principles and Practice in Second Language Acquisition.* New York: Prentice Hall.

Krashen, S. 1984. *Writing: Research, Theory and Application.* Torrance: Laredo.

Krashen, S. 1985a. *The Input Hypothesis: Issues and Implications.* Torrance: Laredo.

Krashen, S. 1985b. *Inquiries and Insights.* Menlo Park: Alemany Press.

Krashen, S. 1987. "Encouraging free reading." In: M. Douglas (Ed.) *Claremont Reading Conference, 51st Yearbook.* Claremont Graduate School: Claremont, California, pp. 1-10.

Krashen, S. 1988. "Do we learn to read by reading? The relationship between free reading and reading ability." In D. Tannen (Ed.) *Linguistics in Context: Connecting Observation and Understanding.* Norwood, New Jersey: Ablex. pp. 269-298.

Krashen, S. 1989a. "We acquire vocabulary and spelling by reading: Additional evidence for the Input Hypothesis." *Modern Language Journal* 73. 440-464.

Krashen, S. 1989b. "Language teaching technology: A low-tech view". *Georgetown University Round Table on Languages and Linguistics.* Washington, D.C.: Georgetown University Press, pp. 393-407.

Krashen, S. 1990. "How reading and writing make you smarter, or how smart people read and write." *Georgetown University Round Table on Languages and Linguistics.* Washington, D.C.: Georgetown University Press. pp. 364-376.

Krashen, S. 1991a. "The input hypothesis: An update." Paper presented at the Georgetown Round Table for Languages and Linguistics. April 3, 1991. Washington, D.C.

Krashen, S. 1991b. "Bilingual education: A focus on current research". National Clearinghouse for Bilingual Education, Occasional Papers in *Bilingual Education*, Spring, 1991k, number 3.

Krashen, S. "Comprehensible input and some competing hypotheses." In R. Courchene, J. Glidden, J. St. John, and C. Therien (Eds.) *Comprehension-Based Language Teaching.* Ottawa: University of Ottawa Press. In press.

Krashen, S., Long, M., and Scarcella, R. 1979. "Age, rate, and eventual attainment in second language acquisition". TESOL *Quarterly* 12: 573-582.

Krashen, S. and Terrell, T. 1983. *The Natural Approach: Language Acquisition in the Classroom.* Menlo Park: Alemany Press.

Krashen, S. and Biber, D. 1988. *On Course: Bilingual Education's Success in California.* Sacramento: California Association for Bilingual Education.

Lafayette, R. and Buscaglia, M. 1985. "Students learn language via a civilization course - a comparison of second language acquisition environments." *Studies in Second Language Acquisition* 7: 323-342.

Lambert, W. and Tucher, G.R. 1972. *The Bilingual Education of Children.* New York: Newbury House.

Langer, J. and Appleby, A. 1987. *How Writing Shapes Thinking.* Urbana, Illinois: National Council of Teachers of English.

Legarreta, D. 1979. "The effects of program models on language acquisition by Spanish-speaking children." TESOL *Quarterly* 13: 521-34.

Linderman, E. 1982. *A Rhetoric for Writing Teachers.* New York: Oxford University Press.

Loughrin-Sacco, S., E. Bommarito, W. Sweet, and A. Beck. 1988. "Anatomy of an elementary French class." Paper presented at the Symposium on Research Perspectives in Adult Language Learning and Acquisition, Ohio State University, October 21, 1988.

Nagy, W., Herman, P., and Anderson, R. 1985. "Learning words from context." *Reading Research Quarterly* 20: 233-253.

Peck, B. 1987. "Spanish for social workers: An intermediate-level communicative course with content lectures." *Modern Language Journal* 71: 402-409.

Pica, T., Young, R., and Doughty, C. 1987. "The impact of interaction on comprehension." TESOL *Quarterly* 21: 737-758.

Ravitch, D. and Finn, C. 1987. *What do Our 17-Year-Olds Know?* New York: Harper and Row.

Rucker, B. 1982. "Magazines and teenage reading skills: Two controlled field experiments." *Journalism Quarterly* 59: 28-33.

Saville-Troike, M. 1984. "What really matters in second language learning for academic achievement?" TESOL *Quarterly* 18: 199-219.

Schleppegrell, M. 1984. "Using input methods to improve writing skills." *System* 12: 42-48.

Shaw, M. 1932. "A comparison of individuals and small groups in the rational solution of complex problems." *American Journal of Psychology* 44: 491-504.

Simon, P. 1980. *The Tongue-Tied American.* New York: Continuum Press.

Simonton, D. 1988. *Scientific Genius: A Psychology of Science. Cambridge:* Harvard University Press.

Slavin, R. 1987. "Cooperative learning and the cooperative school." *Educational Leadership* 45: 7-13.

Slavin, R. 1989-90. "Research on cooperative learning: Consensus and controversy." *Educational Leadership* 47: 52-54.

Smith, F. 1988a. *Understanding Reading.* Hillsdale, New Jersey: Erlbaum. 4th Edition.

Smith, F. 1988b. *Joining the Literacy Club.* Portsmouth, New Hampshire: Heinemann.

Smith, F. 1990.. *To Think..* New York:. Teachers College Press.

Sommers, N. 1980. "Revision strategies of student writers and experienced adult writers." *College Composition and Communication* 31: 378-88.

Sternfeld, S. 1989. "The University of Utah's immersion multiliteracy program: An example of an area studies approach to the design of first-year college foreign language instruction." *Foreign Language Annals* 22: 341-353.

Swain, M. and Lapkin, S. 1982. *Evaluating Bilingual Education: A Canadian Case Study*. Clevedon, Avon, England: Multilingual Matters.

Taylor, D., Berry, P., and

Block, C. 1958. "Does group participation when using brainstorming facilitate or inhibit creative thinking?" *Administrative Science Quarterly* 3:23-47.

Wallas, G. 1926. *The Art of Thought*. London: C.A. Watts (Abridged Version, 1945).

Willig, A. 1985. "A meta-analysis of selected studies on the effectiveness of bilingual education." *Review of Educational Research* 55: 269-317.

Wong-Fillmore, L. 1985. When does teacher-talk work as input? In S. Gass and C. Madden (Eds.) *Input in Second-Language Acquisition*. New York: Newbury House, pp. 17-50.

Young, D. 1990. "An investigation of students' perspectives on anxiety and speaking." *Foreign Language Annals* 23: 539-553.